see
& eat

Helping
to kn
thei

ots

Carmel Houston-Price, Bethany Chapman, Katrina Dulay,
Natalie Ellison, Kate Harvey, Natalie Masento, and David Messer

Published by the University of Reading, Reading, UK
Copyright © University of Reading

University of Reading

ISBN: 978-0-7049160-1-2

All rights reserved. No part of this book may be reproduced or transmitted in any form or by any means, electronic or mechanical, including photocopying, recording, or by any information storage and retrieval system, without permission in writing from the publisher.

SEE & EAT is a trademark.

Design by Fuzzy Flamingo
www.fuzzyflamingo.co.uk

Images used under license from Shutterstock.com

The story of see & eat

The SEE & EAT team are passionate about helping little ones to know and love their vegetables!

We know it can be difficult for parents to persuade young children to eat a variety of vegetables and we have been working hard on ways to make this easier. Research led by Professor Carmel Houston-Price at the University of Reading has shown that pre-schoolers are more likely to eat vegetables at mealtimes if they are already familiar with how the vegetable looks and where it comes from. The more familiar your child is with a food before it appears on their plate, the better… and this is especially true for vegetables they don't like or haven't tried before!

SEE & EAT books are an easy, effective and fun way to introduce children to vegetables before they try them.

SEE & EAT books help children to get to know their vegetables by showing each food's journey 'from farm to fork'. Our research shows that looking at a SEE & EAT picture book with your child for a few minutes each day for a couple of weeks is enough to make a difference. After looking at one of our books, children are often more willing to taste the vegetable than they were beforehand. They eat more of it, and seem to enjoy eating it more, too!

For more information about the research behind SEE & EAT, visit our website at www.research.reading.ac.uk/kids-food-choices

How to use this book to help your little one to know and love carrots!

- Look at this book about carrots with your child for a few minutes every day for a couple of weeks.
- Make reading time fun! Find a time and place to look at the carrot book each day that works best for you and your child. Feel free to look at the book in your own way. You might want to talk about the different sizes of carrots, how they grow, whether you have ever grown or picked carrots yourself, where you usually buy them, or how you like to prepare and eat them. Always be positive about carrots!
- After two weeks, go shopping for carrots with your child, if you can. Point them out in the shop and involve your child in preparing carrots back at home. You might want to try our simple recipes at the end of this book. Then, serve them up. It's time to find out whether your child will crunch on their carrots!
- Remember to chop vegetables into small pieces and to keep an eye on your little ones while they are eating, especially if they are just starting to eat solid foods or the vegetable is new to them.
- Even if they taste just a tiny piece, that is a great start. Don't worry if they refuse to eat it, keep on offering carrots at mealtimes and they are likely to accept them in the end.
- Then it's time to choose another of our vegetable books so that your little one can learn to love another vegetable!

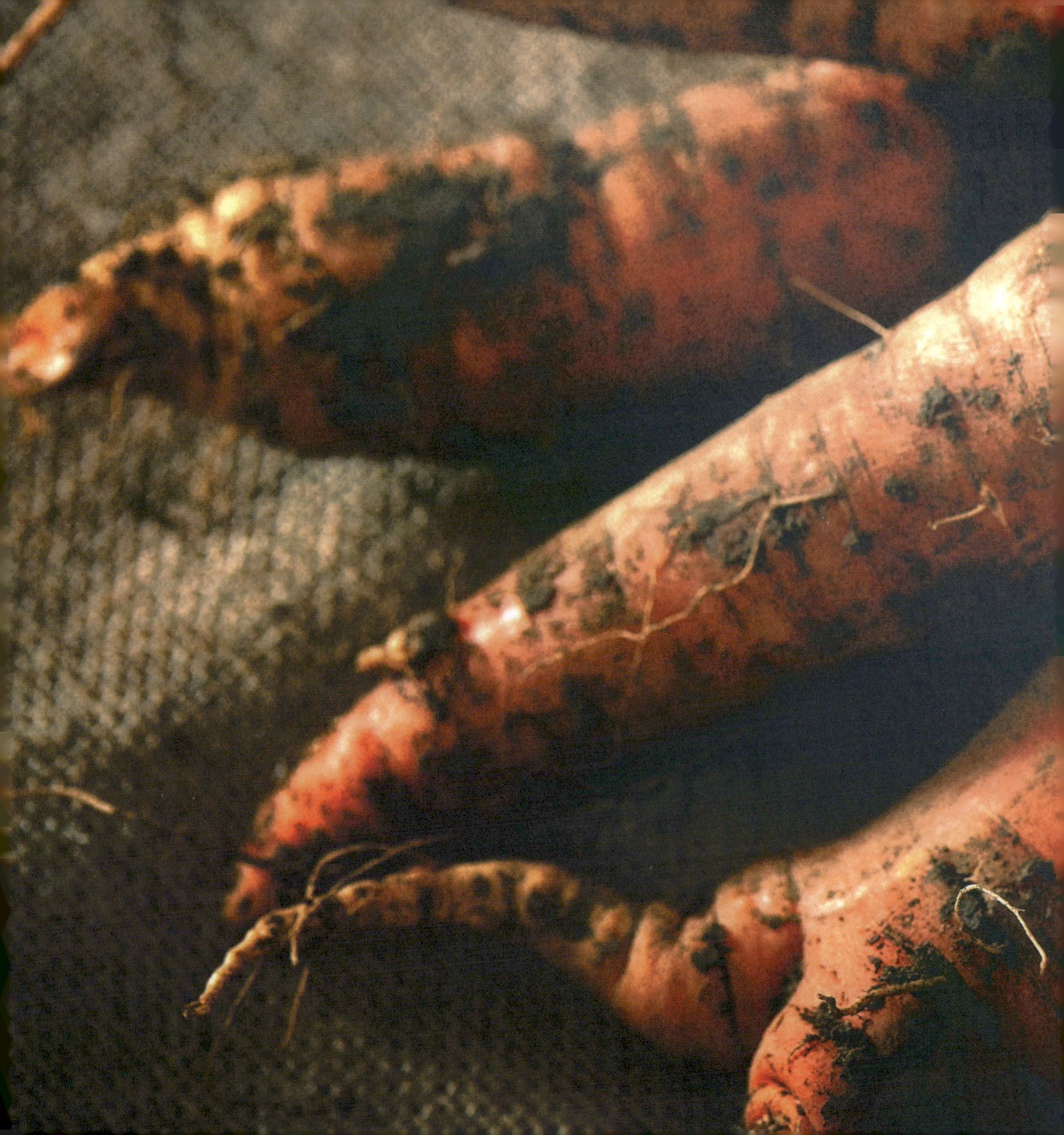

These are carrots.
Carrots are large roots
that we can eat.

Carrots are usually orange, but they can be red, or purple. What colour are the carrots you see here?

Carrots grow underground. They have green wispy leaves that grow above the ground that we call 'fronds'.

It's time to dig up the carrots when the fronds are long and green.

Carrots smell sweet when they are pulled from the earth.

Here are some carrots in a supermarket. The green leaves have been chopped off these carrots.

What is different about these carrots?

At home, we wash carrots to clean them before we eat them.

Sometimes, we peel them and cut them into small pieces.

There are lots of different ways to cook carrots. You can boil, steam, roast or fry them.

Or you can eat carrots raw with a tasty dip. What other vegetables can you eat raw?

Carrots are tasty in soup or served in a vegetable curry.

Which other vegetables can you see in the bowl of curry?

Did you know that you can use carrots to make a tasty cake?

How do YOU like to eat them?

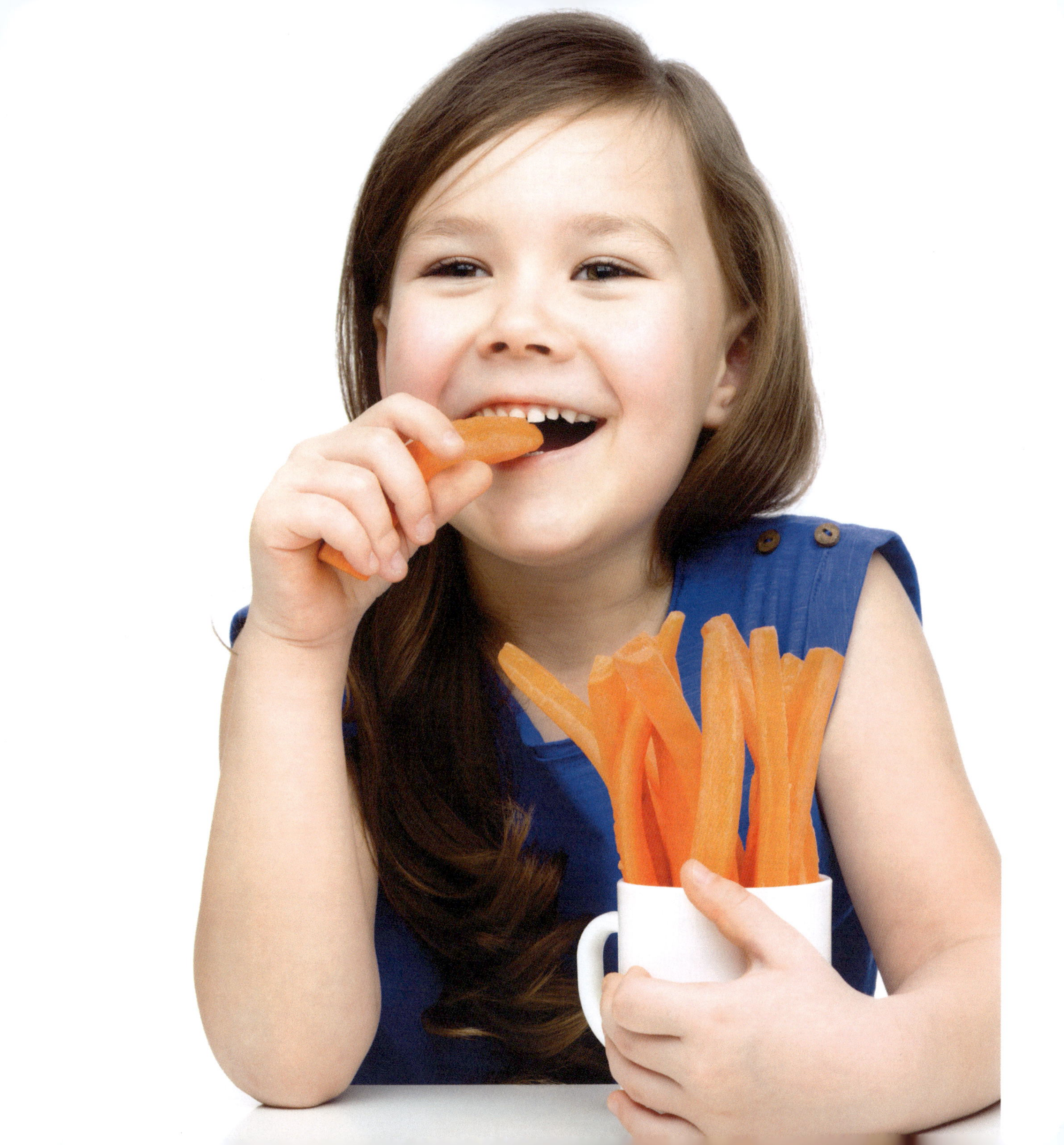

More ideas to help your child to know and love their vegetables!

- Take your child to a farm shop or farmer's market or look out for open days at local farms.
- In the supermarket, let your child find and choose carrots for you, and point out their different colours, shapes and sizes.
- Make up a song about carrots to sing with your child.
- Let your child be your little helper in the kitchen. Choose a simple recipe and talk through the steps. Children can help wash vegetables, put ingredients in a bowl or pass you utensils.
- Encourage your child to explore the look, smell and feel of a carrot by hiding one in a bag alongside other vegetables and playing a guessing game to see if your child can identify them by touch, smell or hearing you describe them.
- Try to ensure that vegetables cover one third of their plate so that your child learns what a healthy plate looks like.
- And remember… it is a good idea to eat together as a family if you can, even if this is just one meal at the weekend. It could be at breakfast, lunch or dinner time – whatever works best for your family.
- Visit our website (www.seeandeat.org) for more activities and games and to download SEE & EAT ebooks.

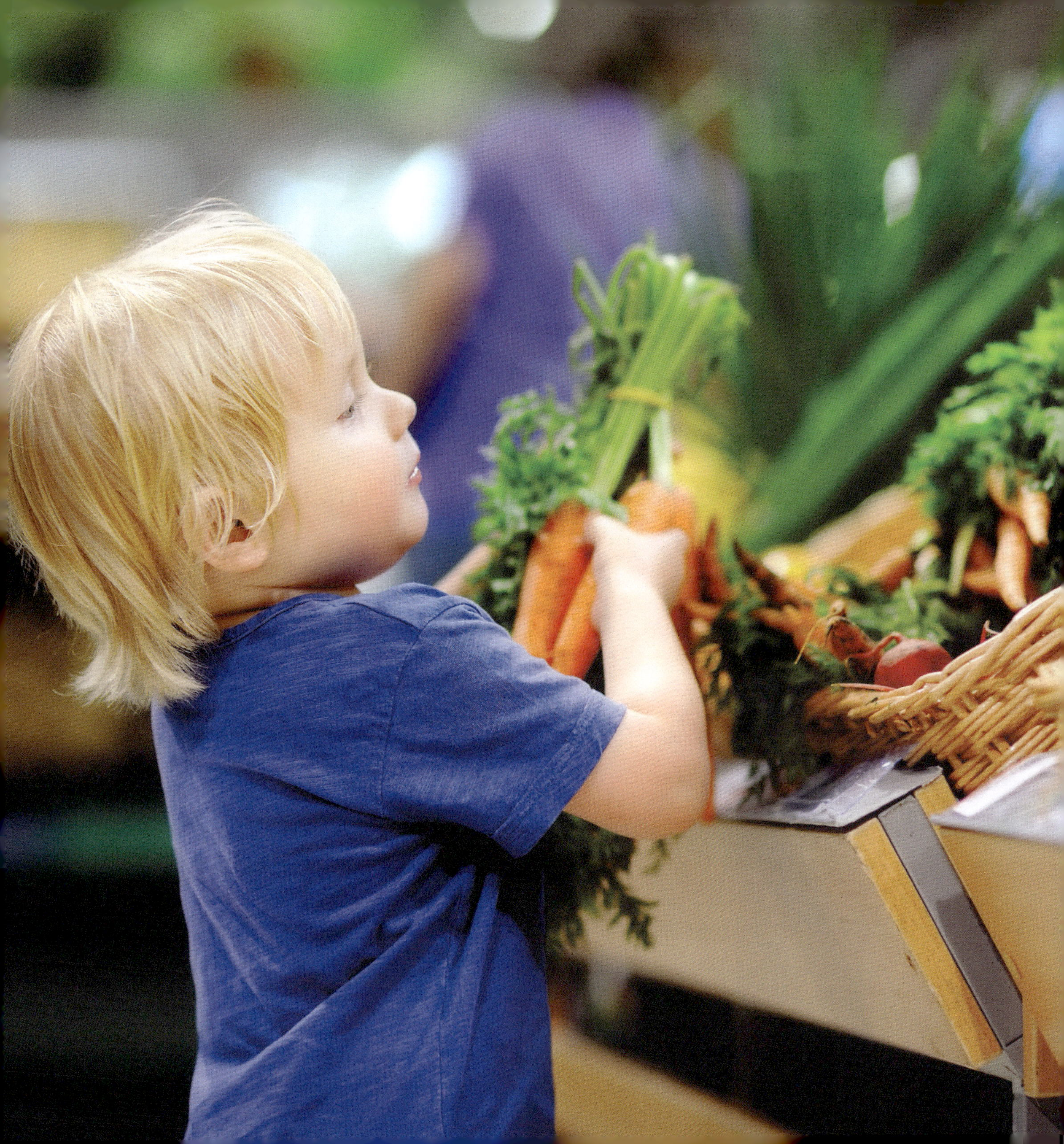

Simple suggestions for preparing carrots

Carrot soup

1. Prepare the carrots by peeling and chopping them into small pieces.
2. Add the carrot pieces to a pan with a pint of vegetable stock.
3. Simmer for 20 minutes, until the carrot is soft.
4. Use a blender to puree the soup until smooth. If you think the soup is too thick, add more stock.
5. Optional – Serve the soup with a swirl of crème fraiche.

Roasted carrots

1. Peel the carrots and quarter them by cutting them into long thin strips.
2. Place the strips on a roasting tray with a dash of oil.
3. Roast them in the oven for 30 minutes until they are crisp on the outside and soft on the inside.

We would love to hear how you get on with the
SEE & EAT books and activities.

Share your stories with us by emailing us at
SeeAndEat@reading.ac.uk

or by contacting the project lead,
Professor Carmel Houston-Price
School of Psychology & Clinical Language Sciences,
University of Reading,
Earley Gate,
Whiteknights,
Reading, UK
RG6 6ES

Acknowledgements

The SEE & EAT team at the University of Reading are indebted to the hundreds of children, parents, teachers and healthcare professionals who have taken part in the research studies, workshops and focus groups that have helped us make SEE & EAT activities as effective as they can be.

We are grateful to EIT Food for funding the work of the SEE & EAT team since 2019. EIT Food is the innovation community for Food of the European Institute of Innovation and Technology (EIT), a body of the EU under Horizon 2020, the EU Framework Programme for Research and Innovation.

We are also grateful to our partners at the Open University, the Universities of Turin, Warsaw and Helsinki, British Nutrition Foundation (BNF) and the European Food Information Council (EUFIC), who have helped to bring SEE & EAT activities to families across Europe.

Finally, we would like to thank Jen Parker at Fuzzy Flamingo (www.fuzzyflamingo.co.uk) for her support with the design and publication of this series of books and Sascha Landskron at Boom House Books (www.boomhousebooks.co.uk) for her enthusiasm for the SEE & EAT project, and for her support with marketing and promotion.

– Professor Carmel Houston-Price & the SEE & EAT team (Dr Bethany Chapman, Lily Clark, Dr Katrina May Dulay, Natalie Ellison, Professor Kate Harvey, Dr Sun Ae Kim, Dr Natalie Masento, Professor David Messer, Dr Alan Roberts)

Look out for the other books in the SEE & EAT series ...

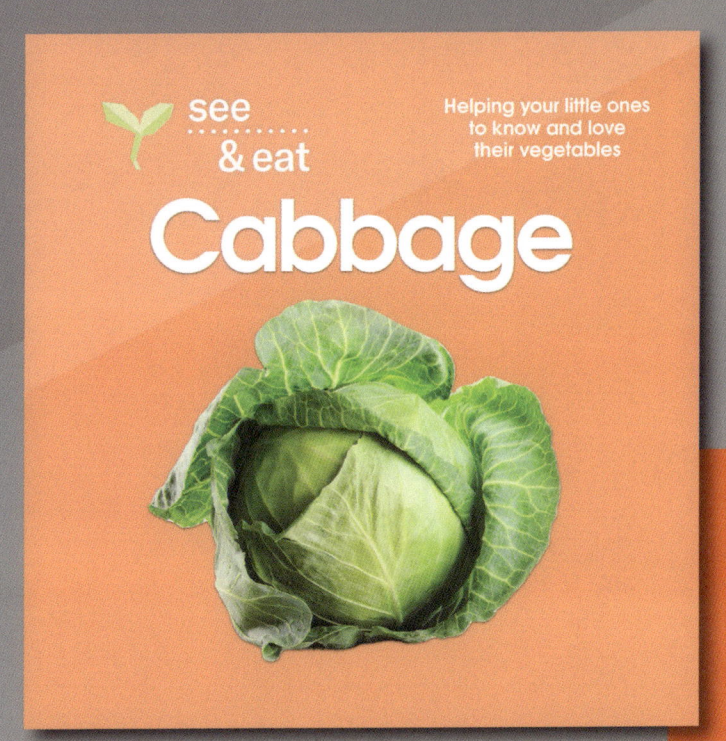

see & eat
Cabbage
Helping your little ones to know and love their vegetables

see & eat
Mushrooms
Helping your little ones to know and love their vegetables

see & eat
Helping your little ones to know and love their vegetables

Peas

see & eat
Helping your little ones to know and love their vegetables

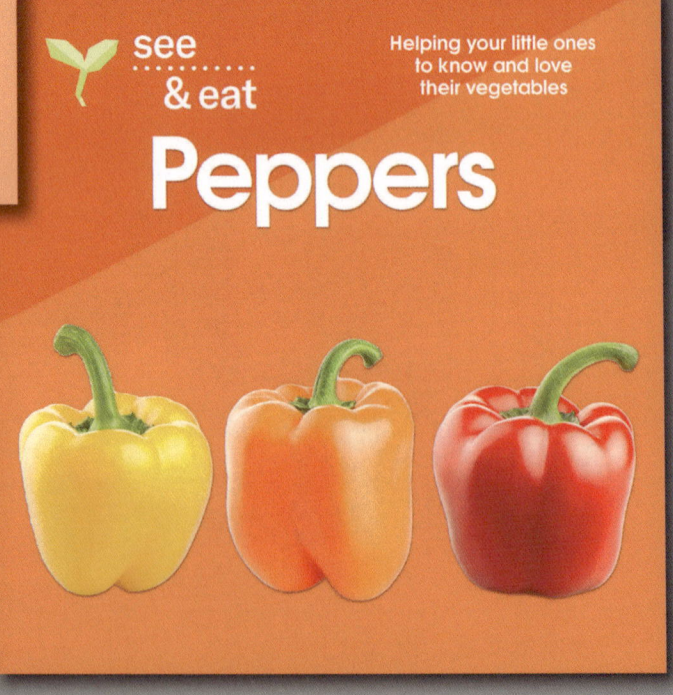

Peppers

… and many more. Visit www.seeandeat.org for the library of ebooks and printed books that are now available in this series.

Printed in Great Britain
by Amazon